Birthday Bear's Book of Birthday Poems

selected by Bobbi Katz
illustrated by Louise Walton and Deborah Borgo

A Care Bear™ Book from Random House, New York

Copyright © 1983 by American Greetings Corporation. Care Bear and Care Bears are trademarks of American Greetings Corporation. All rights reserved under International and Pan-American Copyright Conventions. Published in the United States by Random House, Inc., New York, and simultaneously in Canada by Random House of Canada Limited, Toronto. *Library of Congress Cataloging in Publication Data*: Main entry under title: Birthday bear's book of birthday poems. SUMMARY: The Care Bears present a variety of poems about birthdays. 1. Birthdays—Juvenile poetry. 2. Children's poetry, American. [1. American poetry—Collections. 2. English poetry—Collections. 3. Birthdays—Poetry] I. Katz, Bobbi. PS595.B57B57 1983 811'.54'08033 82-12309 ISBN: 0-394-85658-9 (trade); 0-394-95658-3 (lib. ed.) Manufactured in the United States of America 4 5 6 7 8 9 0

For You on Your Birthday

Three cheers for you! I'm Birthday Bear!
I've come to celebrate
Your very special holiday
On this, your birthday date.
I'll bring a bunch of bright balloons,
I'll sing your birthday song,
And all the other Care Bears
Will help your day along!
This little book of birthday poems
Is the Care Bears' gift for you—
A bouquet of birthday verses
To enjoy the whole year through!

—*Birthday Bear*

Birthday

The next best thing to Christmas,
the next best day to prize
is a birthday, when you're special
in everybody's eyes.

The next best thing to Christmas
if it's summer, spring, or fall,
is a birthday with a party
and a birthday cake and all.

—*Aileen Fisher*

A Birthday

Did you ever think how queer
That, every day all through the year,
Someone has a frosted cake,
And candles for a birthday's sake?

—*Rachel Field*

Oh! To Have a Birthday

Oh! to have a birthday—
Candles burning bright,
Eyes so blue and sparkling,
Happy heart so light!

—*Lois Lenski*

Monday's Child

Monday's child is fair of face,
Tuesday's child is full of grace,
Wednesday's child is full of woe,
Thursday's child has far to go,

Friday's child is loving and giving,
Saturday's child works hard for a living,
And the child that is born on the Sabbath day
Is bonny and blithe, and good and gay.

—Anonymous

The Baby's Name

What should we name our baby?
   We gathered a score of books,
Consulted grandparents, uncles, and aunts,
   Considered the baby's looks.

We didn't like Zephaniah
   Or Matthew or Theodore;
We looked through the family Bible,
   We discussed a hundred or more.

Some were too high-sounding,
   Others were thought too tame;
Some did not seem quite fitting,
   None was the just-right name.

What should we call the baby?
   We argued it, pro and con,
Till at last we reached a final choice,
   And we called the baby John.

—*Tudor Jenks*

Girls' Names

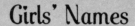

What lovely names for girls there are!
There's Stella like the Evening Star,
And Sylvia like a rustling tree,
And Lola like a melody,
And Flora like a flowery morn,
And Sheila like a field of corn,
And Melusina like the moan
Of water. And there's Joan, like Joan.

—Eleanor Farjeon

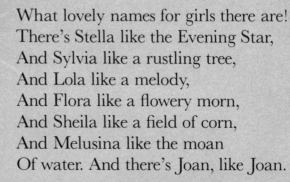

Unfair

It's not fair your parents name you
before you're really YOU—
when you're just some little baby
and ALL you say is "Goo!"
What if you join the circus
and swing from a trapeze?
You wouldn't want some wimpy name
like Prudence, if you please!
What if you are an astronaut
and take a walk in space?
If your parents named you Dolly,
wouldn't you feel out of place?

—*Della Maison*

If We Didn't Have Birthdays

If we didn't have birthdays,
    you wouldn't be you.
If you'd never been born,
    well then what would you do?
If you'd never been born,
    well then what would you be?
You might be a fish!
    Or a toad in a tree!
You might be a doorknob!
    Or three baked potatoes!
You might be a bag full
    of hard green tomatoes.

Or worse than all that . . .
     Why, you might be a WASN'T!
A Wasn't has no fun at all.
     No, he doesn't.
A Wasn't just isn't.
     He just isn't present.
But you . . . You ARE YOU!
     And, now isn't that pleasant!

—*Dr. Seuss*

Someone

There was a boy just one year old
What he said I haven't been told.

There was another and he was two.
He said to the first, "I'm older than you!"

"Ha!" said his sister, who was half-past-three.
"Call *that* old? Just look at me!"

Someone has a birthday and then he's four.
Then he has another and he isn't any more.

Now for a question—Look alive:
How old is Someone? He just turned....

If Someone's five, how long does it last?
And how old is he when it's past?

You can't save the numbers. Time plays tricks.
How old is Someone? He just turned. . . .

Where *do* the birthdays go? Good Heavens!
All the Sixes have turned to. . . .

Someone Seven has a year to wait
And when it's over Someone is. . . .

What's after Eight? That's right! And then?
Right again: Eight . . . Nine . . . and . . . !

—*John Ciardi*

The Wish

Each birthday wish
I've ever made
Really does come true,
Each year I wish
I'll grow some more
And every year
    I
       DO!

—Ann Friday

Birthdays

If birthdays happened once a week
Instead of once a year,
Think of all the gifts you'd get
And all the songs you'd hear.
And think how quickly you'd grow up;
Wouldn't it feel queer
If birthdays happened once a week
Instead of once a year?

—*Mary Ann Hoberman*

What Someone Said When He Was Spanked on the Day Before His Birthday

Some day
I may
Pack my bag and run away.
Some day
I may.
—But not today.

Some night
I might
Slip away in the moonlight.
I might.
Some night.
—But not tonight.

Some night.
Some day.
I might.
I may.
—But right now I think I'll stay.

—John Ciardi

Growing

I'm taller today,
   but nobody knows.
I looked in the mirror
   way up on my toes.
For the very first time
   I saw
   my
   nose.

—*Lilian Moore*

Birthday Puzzle

Where my denim shorts and T-shirt go,
there's a fancy dress with a scratchy bow.
Where my comfy sneakers used to be,
there are shiny shoes that are pinching me.
Mom brushed my hair and made it curl.
Dad said I was his "Birthday Girl."
This is supposed to be MY day,
but I'm not ME when I'm dressed this way.

—Ali Reich

Richer

Beth has some mittens,
but I know they itch her.
Dude has a tea set
with a rosebud pitcher.
Kay has a satin bow
and twenty buttons in a row,
but I have a birthday, so . . .
    I feel richer.

Les has a nugget
he got from a miner.
He also has a fishhook
with a silver shiner.
Cinda has curls, I know,
and dresses made of calico,
but I have a birthday, so . . .
     I feel finer.

—*Aileen Fisher*

Birthday Cake

If little mice have birthdays
(and I suppose they do)

And have a family party
(and guests invited too)

And have a cake with candles
(it would be rather small)

I bet a birthday CHEESE cake
would please them most of all.

—*Aileen Fisher*

Where Is Everyone?

The house is so quiet.
    The day's almost done.
Today is my birthday.
    Where is everyone?
I didn't get a present.
    I didn't get a card.
And no one came over
    to play in the yard.

When I open the door,
    what a treat greets my eyes
As everyone shouts,
    "Happy Birthday!
    SURPRISE!"

—Dorothy Rose

Secrets

If you see a package
Gaily wrapped and tied,
Don't ask too many questions,
'Cause a secret is inside.

—*Elsie Melchert Fowler*

Open the Gift

The ribbons
Won't undo!
My fingers
Don't obey!
The paper's
Stubborn, too,
All sticking
In the way!

—*Regina Sauro*

Birthday Cake

Why is birthday cake so good?
I love it, oh so much!
It's good to eat, but even more
I think it's nice to touch.

It's squoshy white and sticky pink.
It's filled with special goo—
With candy roses on the top.
(One time my piece had two!)

I like to blow the candles out.
I like to make the wish.
But even more I like to lick
The frosting from the dish.

—*Bobbi Katz*

I Never Win at Parties

I never win at parties.
I never win at all.
Someone gets the prizes.
Someone wins the ball.
Someone gets the roses
Off the birthday cake.
I don't get the roses;
I get the stomachache.
Someone pins the tail
On the donkey's seat.
When I pin the donkey,
It ends up on his feet.

Someone drops the clothespins
Right where they should go.
I can't hit the bottle,
Even bending low.
I do not know the reason
Unless it's that I'm small,
Why I don't win at parties.
I just don't win at all.

—*Marci Ridlon*

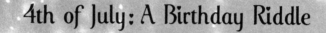

4th of July: A Birthday Riddle

Rockets swoosh and
hiss.
The fireworks begin.

Stars explode and
stream away.
Giant pinwheels
spin.

AAH! Silver flowers
open on the purple
air.

Tall
candles
flare,
showering blue.

It's all
a birthday cake
in the summer sky
for
you-know-who.

—*Lilian Moore*

The Birthday Child

Everything's been different
   All the day long,
Lovely things have happened,
   Nothing has gone wrong.

Nobody has scolded me,
   Everyone has smiled.
Isn't it delicious
   To be a birthday child?

—*Rose Fyleman*

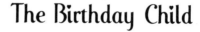

Then

When you can catch
And throw a ball,
And spell
Cat,
Dog,
And Pig,
Then you have finished
Being small
And started
Being Big.

—Dorothy Aldis